Enchanted English

Alison Head

In a cave far away, lives a powerful wizard named Whimstaff. He spends his days finding the answers to ancient English problems and has parchments filled with wonderful words. In this book, Whimstaff shares his knowledge to help you to master the art of English.

Whimstaff has a goblin assistant named Pointy, who is very clever. Pointy helps Whimstaff perfect his spells and gets annoyed with the laziness of Mugly and Bugly, his fat pet frogs. They spend most of their time eating and sleeping and do as little work as possible.

Pointy also helps Whimstaff look after Miss Snufflebeam, a young dragon who is rather clumsy and often loses Whimstaff's words!

Wizard Whimstaff and his friends are very happy solving English problems. Join them on a magical quest to win the Trophy of English Wizardry!

Contents

Haunted Homophones

I'm Miss Snufflebeam and I get very confused! I always get in a muddle with words that are pronounced the same but spelt differently.

pair

pear

I think they are called **homophones**. I often use the wrong word and that can change the meaning of what I'm writing.

Task 1 Can you help me by crossing out the wrong word in each set of brackets? The first one has been done for us.

Spell to shrink a cat's (tail ~~tale~~).

(Too Two) fat frogs and a (great grate) big toad.

A prune squashed flat upon the (rode road).

Fourteen drops of icy (rein rain).

A short, sharp squeeze of tummy (pane pain).

Task 2 My head hurts! I'm sure there are some mistakes in these sentences but I can't find them. Can you underline the mistakes for me?

a Mugly and Bugly gobbled the last peace of cake.

b The magic jumping been hopped off the table.

c Pointy scent Mugly and Bugly to collect flies.

d It is cosy in hour cave.

e Wizard Whimstaff maid a sleeping spell.

f Pointy had scene the spider before.

Task 3

Help! I've muddled up Wizard Whimstaff's pairs of magic homophones. Can you match up the pairs by drawing a line between them?

a law   b there   c strait   d eight   e paw   f you're

straight   ate   lore   your   their   pour

Task 4

Cabradababa! Can you work your magic by making up a sentence for each homophone?

a sauce ______________________

b source ______________________

c tale ______________________

d tail ______________________

e their ______________________

f there ______________________

g hair ______________________

h hare ______________________

Sorcerer's Skill Check

Oops! I've lost the homophones to match these words! Can you write them in for me?

a brake ____________   **b** pail ____________   **c** gait ____________

d matt ____________   **e** our ____________

Super! Time to collect your first silver shield to put on the trophy at the back of the book!

Spellbinding Sequences

Slurp! We're Mugly and Bugly, Pointy's lazy pet frogs! Using a **dictionary** and an **index** is hard work, but it's easier if you learn how to put words into **alphabetical order**. Just look at the first letter of each word

<u>a</u>pple   <u>b</u>ean   <u>c</u>arrot…

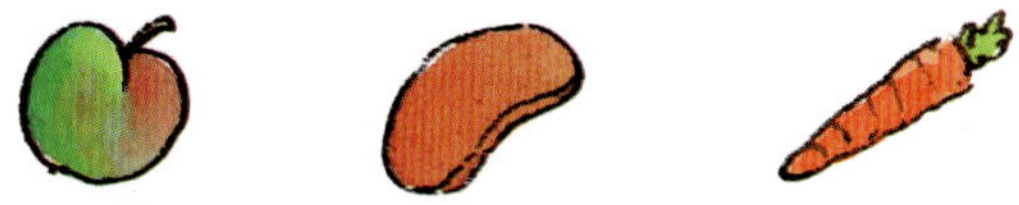

We're off for a snack while you try these.

Task 1 We've eaten some of the letters from this cauldron of alphabet soup. Can you put back the letters we've eaten before Pointy finds out?

a b ☐ d ☐ f g ☐ ☐ j
k l m ☐ o ☐ ☐ r s t
☐ ☐ w x ☐ z

If the first letter's the same you have to look at the next one.

Task 2 Brain cell alert! We're supposed to be arranging Wizard Whimstaff's potions in alphabetical order but we'd rather have a nap.

- Frown Flakes Cereal
- Frightful Face Cream
- Fruity Bat Bubbles
- Freaky Foot Cream
- Dotty Dance Drops

a _____   b _____   c _____   d _____   e _____

Task 3

Croak! Can you help Pointy find the spells he needs? Look at the alphabetical index in the spell book and write down the page number for each spell.

Index

Sparky Spacebugs 2

Spider Soup 4

Spiky Hair Spell 6

Spindly Spread 7

Spinning Eyes Potion 8

Spiny Slugs 9

Spiteful Sauce 11

Squelchy Seaweed 13

Stinky Snakes 14

a Spiteful Sauce ______

b Sparky Spacebugs ______

c Spindly Spread ______

d Stinky Snakes ______

e Spider Soup ______

Sorcerer's Skill Check

We've muddled up Pointy's collection of **w** words. Can you put them on to the scroll in alphabetical order for us? Grub's up!

worn	worry	warning	warlock	wonderful	worms	wart	worst

a ____________________ **e** ____________________

b ____________________ **f** ____________________

c ____________________ **g** ____________________

d ____________________ **h** ____________________

Well done, my apprentice! Collect another silver shield for your trophy!

Vanishing Verbs

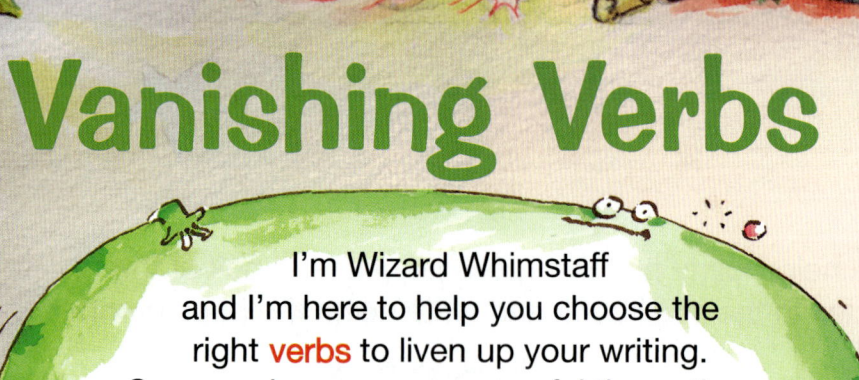

I'm Wizard Whimstaff and I'm here to help you choose the right verbs to liven up your writing. Some verbs are more powerful than others.

It will annoy your parents more if you scream rather than if you just shout.

Task 1 Look at these sentences. Can you underline the verb, then write the sentence again with a more powerful verb chosen from the list?

a The witch climbed onto her broomstick. — swam clambered yawned

____

b The toad jumped into the pond. — relaxed spoke leapt

____

c Miss Snufflebeam ran across the cave. — nibbled dashed brushed

____

d Pointy put the rubbish in the bin. — dragged poured hurled

____

e The spider walked across its web. — scurried danced drove

____

Task 2 My magical verb-invigorating spell turns everyday verbs into powerful verbs. Can you pick a powerful verb from the cauldron to match each of the everyday verbs below?

a sleep ______________

b walk ______________

c fly ______________

d drink ______________

e run ______________

f eat ______________

Task 3

Hey presto! I'd like you to help me organise my collection of powerful verbs. The verbs below mean **walk**, **look** or **drink**. Sort them into the correct jars, then think up one more verb for each.

swig   peep   stroll   stare   hobble   sip

walk	look	drink
______	______	______
______	______	______
______	______	______

Task 4

Can you think of really exciting verbs to fill the gaps in these sentences? Hey presto!

a The owl ________________ down from the branches.

b The troll ________________ down the path.

c The toad ________________ its food.

d The dragon ________________ up the mountain.

Sorcerer's Skill Check

Now, young apprentice, let's see what you know about exciting verbs. Write this sentence again, replacing the verb with a more powerful one from the box.

jumped   scribbled   grabbed   swooped

a Pointy quickly wrote the spell down.

____

b Bugly took the last piece of pizza.

____

My head hurts! You're clever, though! Add another silver shield to your trophy!

Daft Double Consonants

I'm Pointy, Wizard Whimstaff's assistant! Spelling two-syllable words, with a double consonant in the middle, is easy when you know how!

First, think about how you say the **u** sound in the word **bubble**. It has a short sound, so you double the consonant after it.
Now say the word **bugle**. The **u** has a long sound, so the word is spelt with only one **g**. But remember, words which start **mod**, like **modern**, or **model**, don't follow the rule.

Task 1 Say these words out loud, then circle the ones with a short vowel sound. Super!

a happy b butter c written d tiger e grateful
f hopeful g writing h hotter i filler j litter

Task 2 Practice makes perfect! Can you cross out the word in each set of brackets that is spelt incorrectly?

a Miss Snufflebeam was (tapping taping) her feet to the music.

b Wizard Whimstaff was (hoping hopping) the spell would work.

c Pointy wants you to do (supper super) work.

d Mugly and Bugly tucked into their (diner dinner).

e Miss Snufflebeam missed the (comma coma) out of her sentence.

f Pointy was (moping mopping) the floor.

Task 3 Use the pictures to help you fill in the missing words in the spell. Remember the rules for long and short vowel sounds, and double consonants. You'll soon get the hang of it!

Potty Pet Potion

Find a  ______________ wearing mittens,

And a  ______________ in a hat.

Feed a  ______________ to a hippo

And an  ______________ to a cat.

Keep a goldfish in a ladle,

Let your dog sleep on the  ______________,

Climb a  ______________ with an adder

And eat  ______________ with a bat.

Sorcerer's Skill Check

Nearly there! Circle the incorrect spellings in these sentences.

a Wizard Whimstaff started mixxing the pancake batter.

b Miss Snufflebeam was happy playing with her moddel castle.

c The bat hovvered over the holly tree.

d Pointy chose a modern new ketle.

e Mugly and Bugly quickly gobled up their food.

Croak! Grab a silver shield, while we grab a snack!

Amazing Adverbs

Help! I always get in a muddle explaining adverbs. An adverb can tell you more about how an action is done. I think you use them to make your writing more interesting and clearer to people reading it. You can often make adverbs by adding ly to the end of an adjective.

The man's singing was loud.
The man sang loudly.

If the word already ends in y, I think you need to change the y to i, before you add ly.

The owl gave a spooky hoot.
The owl hooted spookily.

Task 1 Help! I've dropped Wizard Whimstaff's spellbook and the words are all muddled up. Can you spot the adverbs and write them back in?

young, bravely, slowly, mild, silent, carefully, quietly, angrily, kind, bold, bad, sadly

a ____________________
b ____________________
c ____________________
d ____________________
e ____________________
f ____________________

Task 2 Oh dear! I'm having a very confusing day! I've covered up the end of these adverbs with my puffs of smoke. Can you write them in again for me?

a The spider scuttled quick ________ across its web.
b The shadow moved creep ________ across the cave.
c The potion bubbled gent ________ in the cauldron.
d The troll stomped off mood ________ .

Task 3 I need to finish these sentences with adverbs made from the adjectives in red. Can you help me?

a Mugly and Bugly are greedy. They eat ______________.

b Pointy is excited when he laughs. He laughs ______________.

c Wizard Whimstaff laughed out loud. He laughed ______________.

d Bugly is lazy. He stretches out ______________.

e Wizard Whimstaff finds it easy to mix new spells. He mixes them ___________.

f Mugly is grumpy. He sulks ______________.

Task 4 My head hurts! Can you help me to write a sentence using each of these adverbs?

a angrily ______________________________

b cheerfully ______________________________

c neatly ______________________________

d sadly ______________________________

e silently ______________________________

f suddenly ______________________________

g gladly ______________________________

Sorcerer's Skill Check

Wizard Whimstaff is going to magic up some **ly** adverbs later. Can you circle the words his spell will work on?

a nervous b spell c rapid d tiny e silent f angry

g furious h wish i kind j bold k mad l obedient

Super work! Stick a silver shield on your trophy!

Sizzling Stories

It's easy to write super stories if you think of them as jigsaw puzzles. Just put the right pieces in the correct places!

- **introduction**: introduces the characters.
- **build-up**: sets the scene for the action.
- **a problem or challenge**: introduces a problem or challenge for the characters.
- **a strong ending**: how the characters solve the problem or meet the challenge.

Now it's time to write your own story!

Task 1 **The introduction.** The introduction is your chance to create really believable characters. Copy this introduction onto a separate piece of paper, choosing words from the brackets to develop your character. Or you could use your own ideas.

(Name) was a (wicked/kind-hearted/eccentric) troll. He lived in a mysterious (castle/swamp/cottage) with his (fierce/tame/dopey) pet (toad/snake/hamster). His hair was (green/pink/white) and (long/spiky/frizzy) and his nose was rather (crooked/large/tiny). He wore (tatty/smart/colourful) clothes and carried a (club/walking stick/umbrella).

Task 2 **The build-up.** Next it's time to set the scene. This second part of the story gets you ready to introduce the problem or challenge in the next section. Think about where you want your character to be and what you want them to be doing. Remember to include any details that will be important for the next section. Choose one of the ideas below, or make up your own.

- The troll tries a magic spell on his pet.
- The troll leaves his pet in charge.
- The troll finds a mysterious box.
- The troll has a visitor.
- The troll loses his pet.

Task 3 **A problem or challenge.** Think of a challenge or problem for the troll to overcome and add it to the other sections of your story. Super! Think carefully about your character and the situation they are in, to make sure the problem is believable and follows on properly.

Remember to include:
- what your character thinks and feels
- powerful verbs and adjectives to describe the action
- a mixture of short and longer sentences for dramatic effect
- important details, but take care not to waffle!

Task 4 **A strong ending.** I can't wait! It's up to you to help your character solve the problem you've just described. You will probably already have an idea of how you want your story to end, so try to add an ending that fits with what we already know about the troll and what's happened so far in the story.

You might want your ending to:
- be based on what we know about the troll and what has happened to him.
- have a surprise or unexpected twist. If so, you still need to make it believable.
- have a moral or message. Maybe the troll learns an important lesson that the reader could also benefit from.

The End!

Sorcerer's Skill Check

Here are some sentences from a story. Can you decide which part in the story they come from?

a He thought nobody had remembered his birthday. ____________

b Pointy is Wizard Whimstaff's assistant. ____________

c It was his birthday. ____________

d His friends surprised him with a party. ____________

Croak! Seeing you do all that work has made us tired! Take another silver shield while we take a nap!

Apprentice Wizard Challenge 1

Challenge 1 These words are homophones. Can you think of the matching word?

a weight ____________________

b piece ____________________

c reed ____________________

d wrap ____________________

e waste ____________________

Challenge 2 Can you write these words again in alphabetical order?

wise white which wizard wicked witch wish

a ____________________

b ____________________

c ____________________

d ____________________

e ____________________

f ____________________

g ____________________

Challenge 3 Write down a more powerful verb for each of these.

a shout ____________________

b hold ____________________

c eat ____________________

d laugh ____________________

e hit ____________________

f walk ____________________

g drink ____________________

Challenge 4 Can you cross out the incorrect spelling in each pair?

a jely jelly **b** ladder lader **c** table tabble

d funy funny **e** ripple riple

Challenge 5 Draw a line to match these verbs with an appropriate adverb.

a to run	hungrily
b to tiptoe	quickly
c to shout	gently
d to touch	quietly
e to eat	angrily

Challenge 6 Can you decide where in the story these sentences belong; the introduction, the build-up, the problem, or the ending?

a One day, Wizard Whimstaff left Miss Snufflebeam alone in the cave. ____________

b Wizard Whimstaff had to make a new spell to put it right. ____________

c Miss Snufflebeam is a little, red dragon. ____________

d She dropped a bottle of spotty spell that made everything spotty. ____________

Count how many challenges you got right and put stars on the test tube to show your score. Then have a silver shield for your trophy!

Super Suffixes

Now, my apprentice,
it's time to learn how you can **add suffixes to nouns and verbs to make adjectives**. Suffixes are collections of letters added to the end of a word. Suffixes like **ly**, **able**, **ing**, **ful**, **like**, **ic** and **worthy** can often be added to nouns to make adjectives.

hope + ful = hopeful

Now you try! Just do the best you can.

Task 1 Can you choose the right suffix from the cauldron to complete these word sums?

a ghost + ____________ =

b manage + ____________ =

c hero + ____________ =

d hate + ____________ =

e trust + ____________ =

Task 2 Allakazan! Can you write down an adjective that can be made by adding a suffix to each of these nouns and verbs?

a child	____________	**f** cost	____________
b shock	____________	**g** fear	____________
c hope	____________	**h** laugh	____________
d angel	____________	**i** tune	____________
e help	____________	**j** depend	____________

Task 3 Listen carefully. The right suffix to choose depends on the rest of the sentence. Can you cross out the wrong adjective from each set of brackets?

a The black cat's kittens were (~~playable~~ playful).

b The apprentice was (trustworthy trustable).

c Miss Snufflebeam's dream was (wishful wishworthy).

d The poor man was (penniful penniless).

e The spaceman was (weightly weightless).

Task 4 Wave a magic wand to turn these nouns or verbs into adjectives.

a The old car was not road ________________.

b The wizard's cloak was wash ________________.

c It was a wonder ________________ night.

d The woman stroked her faith ________________ cat.

e The magic mirror was unbreak ________________.

Sorcerer's Skill Check

Abracadabra! I'm going to use my magic to turn these nouns and verbs into adjectives. Can you work out which list they should go into?

fret shock break hope dread alarm drink bend gall

able	ful	ing
________	________	________
________	________	________
________	________	________

Dabracababra! Yet another silver shield!

Agitated Adjectives

It's easy to make your writing magical if you choose the right **adjectives**. Some are more powerful than others.

For example, **hilarious** is more powerful than **amusing**. Now you try!

Task 1

Super! My magic chart measures the strength of adjectives. Can you fill in the gaps it has left with adjectives from the lists below?

small huge microscopic	hot warm cold freezing	dry drenched damp wet moist

a	b	c
______	boiling	______
large	______	______
medium	______	______
______	cool	______
tiny	______	______
______	______	parched

Task 2

Now let's see if you can use **er** and **est** to make sense of these sentences! You'll soon get the hang of it!

a Because they are greedy, Mugly and Bugly always take the bigg______ slice of cake they can find.

b Only the small______ mouse would fit through the tiny hole.

c The spider grew fatt______ every day.

d The smaller potion bottle was too small, as was the middle-sized one. But the larg______ one was just right.

e The frog jumped high______ than ever before.

Task 3

Adding adverbs to adjectives is easy when you know how! Draw lines to match the pairs of words to the correct part of the picture. Practice makes perfect!

a very happy

quite happy

b very high

quite high

c quite colourful more colourful

very colourful most colourful

Task 4

Can you think of stronger adjectives to replace the ones in brackets?

a Miss Snufflebeam was (frightened) of the dark. ____________

b Pointy's cooking was (tasty). ____________

c Mugly gave a (loud) croak. ____________

d Wizard Whimstaff was (angry) with Mugly and Bugly. ____________

e Bugly complained that he was (hungry). ____________

Sorcerer's Skill Check

Can you sprinkle magic dust on these sentences and write them out again, making them as gripping as possible? Just pick the strongest option from the brackets to work your magic!

a The cauldron was (warm/hot/scalding).

____

b The monster was (quite/very/extremely) scary.

____

c Pointy looked into the (biggish/bigger/biggest) crystal ball.

____

Croak! Time for another silver shield, clever clogs!

Possessive Apostrophes

We use **apostrophes** to show when something belongs to someone or to a group. Just follow the rules to make sure you always put the apostrophe in the right place.

With **single or collective nouns** the apostrophe appears **before the s**

the cat's tail the people's houses.

When **plurals end with s**, the apostrophe appears **after the s**

the cats' tails or the girls' hats.

With **its**, there is no apostrophe to mark possession. The only time an apostrophe appears in **it's** is to tell you that it has been shortened from **it is**.

The dog licked its bowl. It's empty now.

Task 1

Can you use the pictures to help fill in the gaps in these sentences? Remember to look at whether the sentence is talking about one person or animal, or several.

a The ____________ whiskers are blue.

b The ____________ broomstick is broken.

c The fly flew into the ____________ webs.

d The ____________ lily pad was slimy, so he jumped off.

Task 2

Well done, young apprentice! Now use the plural machine to change these singulars. The first one has been done for you.

a the girl's toy — the girls' toys

b the man's bag — ____________

c the dog's basket — ____________

d the child's shoes — ____________

e the dragon's tail — ____________

Task 3 Abracadabra! Can you fill in these gaps with its or it's?

a The cat twitched __________ whiskers.

b __________ spooky in the cave.

c The spell must be cast before __________ light.

d The snail hid in __________ shell.

e The dragon went off on __________ own.

f The spider repaired __________ web.

Task 4 The apostrophes have been missed out of this piece of writing. Can you put them in? Just do the best you can.

Its a wet night. The bird takes cover in a cave and finds Wizard Whimstaffs friends inside. Miss Snufflebeams puffs of smoke fill the air and its not long before everyone needs some fresh air. The bird sees the rain has stopped, so its time to fly away.

Sorcerer's Skill Check

Let's see what you've learnt about possessive apostrophes. Can you rewrite these sentences? Allakazan! I've done the first one for you.

a The hats of the witches. The witches' hats.

b The hat of the wizard. __________

c The magic of the spell. __________

d The secrets of the children. __________

e The wings of the bats. __________

Practice made perfect! Pop another silver shield on your trophy!

Repulsive Reports

Slurp!
Reports about things that have happened need to tell the reader exactly what happened and in what order. You need to be careful to be accurate and make sure the words you use keep it interesting for the reader. Sounds too much like hard work to us!

Task 1 Miss Snufflebeam has had an accident in the cave. Can you unscramble her report of what happened while we have a nap? Number the sections to put them in order.

a I turned around to look. ________

b I was busy mixing potions in the cave. ________

c Then my tail knocked the bottles over. ________

d They hit the floor and broke. ________

e Suddenly I heard a noise behind me. ________

Task 2 Croak! Connectives are the words and phrases we use to link events in a report. They make it interesting to read and help the reader to understand the order of events. While we have a snack, pick connectives to fill the gaps in these sentences.

Remember that connectives can be useful but shouldn't be used more than once or twice!

Then   Next   after that   Eventually   Finally

It was a wet Wednesday afternoon. Mugly and Bugly were hungry so they ate some pizza. ________________ they ate a large slice of cake. ________________, they ate three pies and ________________ some ice cream. ________________ they ate a whole packet of biscuits. ________________, they were full.

Task 3

Brain cell alert! When you're reporting events you need to be as accurate as possible. Look at the pictures and then try to spot the mistakes in the report. Circle each mistake as you find it.

It was a sunny day. The bat was hanging from a tree, asleep. Then the bat woke up and saw a man walking by. He was wearing a blue hat and carrying a red umbrella. Next, the bat flew down, grabbed the umbrella and flew away with it.

Task 4

Grub's up! We're supposed to be writing a report based on this page from Wizard Whimstaff's diary. Will you do it for us on a separate piece of paper, while we have a snack? Try to use the connectives from the box.

first	after that	then	eventually	finally	next

7.30	Got up and got dressed
7.45	Had breakfast (poached snakes' eggs)
8.00	Went for a walk with Pointy
9.00	Worked on a difficult new spell
12.00	Had lunch with Miss Snufflebeam
1.00	Went for a ride on the broomstick

Wizard Whimstaff

Sorcerer's Skill Check

Slurp! We want to know if you've been paying attention. Answer true or false to these questions about the report you've just written.

a Wizard Whimstaff had dragons' eggs for breakfast. ____________

b Wizard Whimstaff went for a walk after lunch. ____________

c After lunch Wizard Whimstaff went for a ride on the broomstick. ____________

d Wizard Whimstaff had lunch with Pointy. ____________

Allakazan! Magic yourself another shield!

Inspiring Instructions

Oh dear!
I'm trying to build a model of an enchanted castle but the instructions aren't very clear! I'm getting in a muddle. I think instructions need to be written clearly so the reader knows exactly what they need to do and in what order. Can you help me work these out?

Task 1 My head hurts! I can remember that good instructions use very powerful verbs called **imperative verbs**, to tell the readers what to do. Here are the instructions for the base of my model. Can you underline the imperative verbs?

a Cut out the pieces.

b Fold along the dotted lines.

c Join the two pieces together with glue.

d Attach the trim.

e When the glue is dry, paint the model.

Task 2 Help! I'm not sure how to build the main castle keep! One way to make it clearer is for each step to be labelled with a number or letter. Can you re-write these instructions on the parchment, separating the different tasks and numbering them?

Press out the wall sections. Fold along the dotted lines and join the two sections with glue. Paint the walls. Assemble the roof and attach to the walls. Varnish the model. Apply a second coat of varnish.

Task 3 Abracadada! Now I'm ready to put the castle keep and the base together. Can you add connective words from the box to help me decide what to do first?

Before you start	Next	First	Finally	then	When the glue is dry

______________, make sure that all glue and paint is dry. ________ place the keep onto the base, ________ carefully glue the keep in place. ________ add the drawbridge. ________ ______________ paint in the moat. ________ add the model knights to the castle.

Sorcerer's Skill Check

glue	cut out	paint	wait

Oh dear! I want to make a model stagecoach to go with my castle, but the instructions are muddled up and bits are missing. Can you add the missing imperative verbs from the box, then number the instructions to put them in order?

a ________ the sections together. ☐

b Using sharp scissors, carefully ________ the model pieces. ☐

c ________ the finished model blue. ☐

d ________ for the glue to dry. ☐

Brain cell alert! Have another silver shield while we have a snooze...

Powerful Punctuation

Punctuation
helps readers make sense of your writing. Here's what you need to know:

Pointy's Punctuation Pointers

- *At the end of a sentence, use a full stop; a question mark for a question; or an exclamation mark to indicate strong feelings like shock or surprise.*
- *To tell the reader to pause, use a comma.*
- *Speech marks come before and after bits of direct speech – that means when someone is actually talking.*

It's easy when you know how!

Task 1

Some of Wizard Whimstaff's magic commas are hiding in this piece of writing. Can you circle the commas that shouldn't be there? Practice makes perfect!

To make a rabbit appear, use the magic, wishing spell. Use fairy dust, moonbeams and, magic beans. Mix well, then use, a magic wand to make the spell. Say the magic words and the, rabbit will appear.

Task 2

Super! I've been too tidy and put all the full stops, question marks and exclamation marks from the ends of these sentences into bottles. Can you put them back?

a Miss Snufflebeam is rather clumsy

b Where is the secret cave

c The fireworks were amazing

d Mugly and Bugly are pet frogs

e When will Pointy be back

f How frightening

g What time is it

h Boo

Task 3 Some of the speech marks from these sentences have disappeared behind Wizard Whimstaff's hat! Can you write them back in?

a “Fetch the cauldron , said Wizard Whimstaff.

b Help!” said Miss Snufflebeam.

c “Just do the best you can , said Wizard Whimstaff.

d Slurp!” said Mugly and Bugly.

e “Where's my hat ? asked Pointy.

Task 4 Now you try. Can you write a sentence using each of the groups of punctuation marks below?

a “ ” ! ________________________________

b , . ________________________________

c , ! ________________________________

d “ ” ? ________________________________

Sorcerer's Skill Check

One exercise to go! In the jars are the rest of the punctuation marks I've collected. Can you fit them into the gaps in these sentences?

, , ? !

a On the table was a wand, a hat____ a cauldron and a cape.

b Which potion will make Pointy invisible____

c “Super____” said Pointy.

d It was a dark____ gloomy night.

Another silver shield for a fine apprentice!

Apprentice Wizard Challenge 2

Challenge 1

Choose suffixes from the cauldron to change these nouns into adjectives. Some are used more then once.

- **a** magic________
- **b** force________
- **c** seed________
- **d** cream________
- **e** hero________
- **f** dream________
- **g** glee________
- **h** need________

Challenge 2

Can you put these adjectives in order of intensity, starting with the word in red?

- **a** tasty delicious bland ____________________
- **b** thin skinny slim ____________________
- **c** medium huge large ____________________
- **d** freezing cold cool ____________________
- **e** happy overjoyed delighted ____________________
- **f** bigger biggest big ____________________
- **g** longer longest long ____________________

Challenge 3

Can you turn these possessive singulars into plurals by putting the apostrophe in the right place?

- **a** dog's bowl ____________________
- **b** mouse's cheese ____________________
- **c** man's hat ____________________
- **d** bat's wings ____________________
- **e** cat's whiskers ____________________

Challenge 4 Underline the connective words and phrases in this short report.

On Tuesday morning it started to rain. First of all it was just drizzle, then it got heavier. In the end it was pouring down. Eventually it stopped but there were puddles everywhere.

Challenge 5 Can you split these instructions into numbered steps? Write your version in the space below.

Weigh out the ingredients. Mix the butter and sugar. Add the eggs and beat well. Fold in the flour. Bake in a hot oven. When cooked, leave to cool. Decorate with icing.

a ______________________________

b ______________________________

c ______________________________

d ______________________________

e ______________________________

f ______________________________

g ______________________________

Challenge 6 The punctuation marks have been left out of this piece of writing. Can you add them in?

I've collected a snake's tooth an eagle's feather a lizard's claw and a bat's wing for the spell said Miss Snufflebeam Help Where is the spell book Here it is said Pointy Wow Do you really need all these ingredients for the spell

Count how many challenges you got right and put stars on the test tube to show your score. Then take the last silver shield for your trophy!

Answers

Pages 2–3

Task 1 The following words are incorrect: tale, too, grate, rode, rein, pane.

Task 2 The following words are incorrect:

a peace	(piece)
b been	(bean)
c scent	(sent)
d hour	(our)
e maid	(made)
f scene	(seen)

Task 3
a law, lore
b there, their
c strait, straight
d eight, ate
e paw, pour
f you're, your

Task 4 Many answers are possible.

Sorcerer's Skill Check
a break
b pale
c gate
d mat
e hour

Pages 4–5

Task 1 a b c d e f g h i j k l m n o p q r s t u v w x y z

Task 2
a Dotty Dance Drops
b Freaky Foot Cream
c Frightful Face Cream
d Frown Flakes Cereal
e Fruity Bat Bubbles

Task 3
a 11
b 2
c 7
d 14
e 4

Sorcerer's Skill Check
a warlock
b warning
c wart
d wonderful
e worms
f worn
g worry
h worst

Pages 6–7

Task 1
a climbed
The witch clambered onto her broomstick.
b jumped
The toad leapt into the pond.
c ran
Miss Snufflebeam dashed across the cave.
d put
Pointy hurled the rubbish in the bin.
e walked
The spider scurried across its web.

Task 2
a snooze
b saunter
c swoop
d guzzle
e sprint
f munch

Task 3

Walk	Look	Drink
stroll	peep	swig
hobble	stare	sip

other possible answers are:

amble	gaze	swallow
limp	examine	guzzle

Task 4 Many answers are possible.

Sorcerer's Skill Check
a Pointy scribbled the spell down.
b Bugly grabbed the last piece of pizza.

Pages 8–9

Task 1 The following have a short vowel sound:
a happy
b butter
c written
h hotter
i filler
j litter

Task 2 The following words are incorrect:
a taping
b hopping
c supper
d diner
e coma
f moping

Task 3 The missing words appear in this order: kitten, rabbit, carrot, apple, table, ladder, jelly.

Sorcerer's Skills Check
The following words are spelt incorrectly:
a mixing
b model
c hovered
d kettle
e gobbled

Pages 10–11

Task 1 The adverbs are: slowly, angrily, bravely, carefully, quietly, sadly.

Task 2
a quickly
b creepily
c gently
d moodily

Task 3
a greedily
b excitedly
c loudly
d lazily
e easily
f grumpily

Task 4 Many answers are possible.

Sorcerer's Skill Check
The spell will work on these words:
a nervous
c rapid
e silent
f angry
g furious
i kind
j bold
k mad
l obedient

Pages 12–13

Tasks 1–4 Many answers are possible.

Sorcerer's Skill Check
a Problem or challenge
b Introduction
c Build-up
d Ending

Pages 14–15

Challenge 1
a wait
b peace
c read
d rap
e waist

Challenge 2
a which
b white
c wicked
d wise
e wish
f witch
g wizard

Challenge 3
Several answers are possible.

Challenge 4
The following spellings are incorrect:
a jely
b lader
c tabble
d funy
e riple

Challenge 5
a to run quickly
b to tiptoe quietly
c to shout angrily
d to touch gently
e to eat hungrily

Challenge 6
a Build-up
b Ending
c Introduction
d Problem or Challenge

Pages 16–17

Task 1
a ghost + ly = ghostly
b manage + able = manageable
c hero + ic = heroic
d hate + ful = hateful
e trust + worthy = trustworthy

Task 2
a childlike, childish
b shocking, shockable
c hopeful
d angelic
e helpful
f costly
g fearful
h laughable, laughing
i tuneful
j dependable

Task 3 The following adjectives are incorrect:
a playable
b trustable
c wishworthy
d penniful
e weightly

Task 4
a roadworthy
b washable
c wonderful
d faithful
e unbreakable

Sorcerer's Skill Check

able	ful	ing
bend	hope	shock
break	dread	alarm
drink	fret	gall

Pages 18–19

Task 1

a	b	c
huge	boiling	drenched
large	hot	wet
medium	warm	moist
small	cool	damp
tiny	cold	dry
microscopic	freezing	parched

Task 2
a biggest
b smallest
c fatter
d largest
e higher

Task 3

a very happy

quite happy

b very high

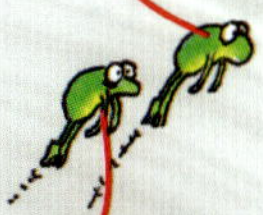

quite high

c quite colourful more colourful

very colourful most colourful

Task 4 Many answers are possible.

Sorcerer's Skill Check

a scalding
b extremely
c biggest

Page 20–21

Task 1 **a** cat's **b** wizard's
c spiders' **d** frog's

Task 2 **a** the girls' toys
b the men's bags
c the dogs' baskets
d the children's shoes
e the dragons' tails

Task 3 **a** its
b It's
c it's
d its
e its
f its

Task 4 It's a wet night. The bird takes cover in a cave and finds Wizard Whimstaff's friends inside. Miss Snufflebeam's puffs of smoke fill the air and it's not long before everyone needs some fresh air. The bird sees the rain has stopped, so it's time to fly away.

Sorcerer's Skill Check

a The witches' hats
b The wizard's hat
c The spell's magic
d The children's secrets
e The bats' wings

Pages 22–23

Task 1 **a** 3 **d** 5
b 1 **e** 2
c 4

Task 2 It was a wet Wednesday afternoon. Mugly and Bugly were hungry so they ate some pizza. Then they ate a large slice of cake. Next, they ate three pies and after that some ice cream. Finally they ate a whole packet of biscuits. Eventually, they were full.

Task 3 It was a rainy day. The bat was hanging from a tree, asleep. Then the bat woke up and saw a woman walking by. She was wearing a red hat and carrying a yellow umbrella. Next, the bat flew down, grabbed the hat and flew away with it.

Task 4 Many answers are possible.

Sorcerer's Skill Check

a false **b** false
c true **d** false

Pages 24–25

Task 1 Cut out the pieces.
Fold along the dotted lines.
Join the two pieces together with glue.
Attach the trim.
When the glue is dry, paint the model.

Task 2 **1** Press out the wall sections.
2 Fold along the dotted lines and join the two sections with glue.
3 Paint the walls.
4 Assemble the roof and attach to the walls.
5 Varnish the model.
6 Apply a second coat of varnish.

Task 3 Before you start, make sure that all glue and paint is dry. First place the keep onto the base, then carefully glue the keep in place. Next add the drawbridge. When the glue is dry paint in the moat. Finally add the model knights to the castle.

Sorcerer's Skill Check

a glue (**2**) **b** cut out (**1**)
c paint (**4**) **d** wait (**3**)

Pages 26–27

Task 1 To make a rabbit appear, use the magic, wishing spell. Use fairy dust, moonbeams and, magic beans. Mix well, then use, a magic wand to make the spell. Say the magic words and the, rabbit will appear.

Task 2 **a** . **e** ?
b ? **f** !
c ! **g** ?
d . **h** !

Task 3 **a** "Fetch the cauldron," said Wizard Whimstaff.
b "Help!" said Miss Snufflebeam.
c "Just do the best you can," said Wizard Whimstaff.
d "Slurp!" said Mugly and Bugly.
e "Where's my hat?" asked Pointy.

Task 4 Many answers are possible.

Sorcerer's Skill Check

a , **b** ?
c ! **d** ,

Pages 28–29

Challenge 1

a magical **e** heroic
b forceful **f** dreamy, dreamless
c seedless **g** gleeful
d creamy **h** needless, needy, needful

Challenge 2

a bland, tasty, delicious
b slim, thin, skinny
c medium, large, huge
d cool, cold, freezing
e happy, delighted, overjoyed
f big, bigger, biggest
g long, longer, longest

Challenge 3

a dogs' **d** bats'
b mice's **e** cats'
c men's

Challenge 4

On Tuesday morning it started to rain. First of all it was just drizzle, then it got heavier. In the end it was pouring down. Eventually it stopped but there were puddles everywhere.

Challenge 5

1 Weigh out the ingredients.
2 Mix the butter and sugar.
3 Add the eggs and beat well.
4 Fold in the flour.
5 Bake in a hot oven.
6 When cooked, leave to cool.
7 Decorate with icing.

Challenge 6

"I've collected a snake's tooth, an eagle's feather, a lizard's claw and a bat's wing for the spell," said Miss Snufflebeam. "Help! Where is the spell book?"
"Here it is," said Pointy. "Wow! Do you really need all these ingredients for the spell?"

The end

Wizard's Trophy of Excellence

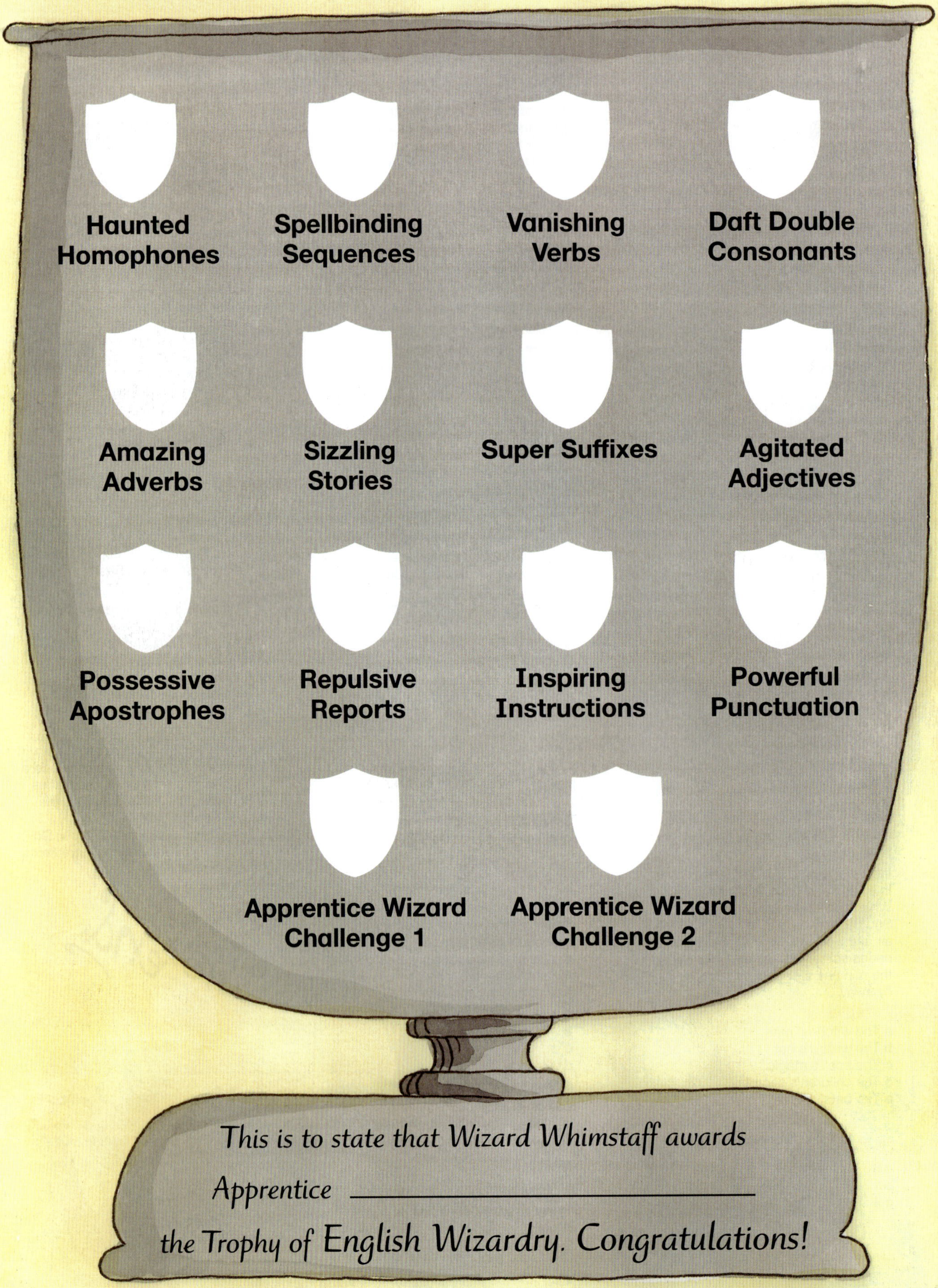